Fun with Fractions

Patricia J. Murphy

Rosen Classroom Books & Materials
New York

Published in 2003 by The Rosen Publishing Group, Inc.
29 East 21st Street, New York, NY 10010

Book Design: Haley Wilson

Photo Credits: Cover, pp. 1, 5, 6, 9, 10, 11 (pies), 12 by Haley Wilson; p. 4 © The Image Bank; pp. 7, 11 © David Young-Wolff/PhotoEdit/ PictureQuest; p. 8 © FPG International; p. 13 © PhotoDisc; p. 14 © Kelly-Mooney Photography/Corbis.

ISBN: 0-8239-6376-4
6-pack ISBN: 0-8239-9558-5

Manufactured in the United States of America

Contents

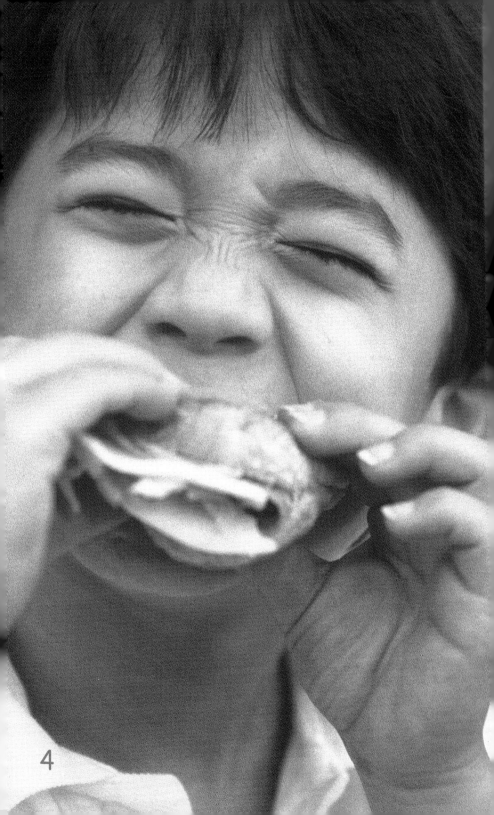

What Are Fractions?

Fractions are parts of things. Everything is made of parts. The parts of something make up its **whole**.

When you eat 1/2 (one-half) of a sandwich, you eat one of its two parts. Two parts make up your whole sandwich.

If Cindy cuts her sandwich into two halves, how many halves must she eat to finish the whole sandwich? The answer is two.

Name That Fraction!

The top number of a fraction tells how many parts of the whole you are talking about. The bottom number tells how many **equal** parts are in the whole.

When Brad drank 1/4 (one-quarter) of his milk, he drank one part out of the four equal parts in the whole.

If Brad drinks 3/4 (three-quarters) of his milk, he drinks three parts out of the four equal parts in the whole.

Sets, Groups, and Fractions

Fractions can also help us talk about things in a group or **set**. We can use fractions to show how many things in a set are alike in some way.

Ann has three books. One out of the three books, or 1/3 (one-third) of the books, is yellow. Two out of the three books, or 2/3 (two-thirds) of the books, are red.

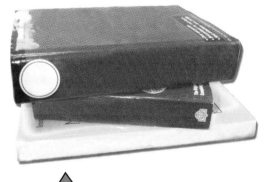

▲

How many books in the group are yellow? Answer: One out of the three, or 1/3.

Equal Fractions

Some fractions may look different even when they are really the same. They are called equal fractions. "Equal" means the same.

Joanne baked three pies. Erik ate 2/4 (two-quarters) of the cherry pie. Kerri ate 4/8 (four-eighths) of the pumpkin pie. Don ate 1/2 of the apple pie. They all ate the same amount of pie! The fractions 2/4, 4/8, and 1/2 are equal fractions.

If Joanne cuts a pumpkin pie into 10 parts, how many pieces must she eat to have 1/2 of the pie? The answer is 5.

10

2/4

1/2

11

Why Do We Use Fractions?

We use fractions in many ways. Fractions help us **measure** things.  The plant in this picture is 6 inches or 1/2 of a foot tall.

6 inches = 1/2 foot

Fractions also help us count money. A quarter is 1/4 of a dollar. That means there are four quarters in a dollar. A dime is 1/10 (one-tenth) of a dollar. That means there are ten dimes in a dollar.

Fractions can also help us tell time. There are sixty minutes in an hour. That means that 1/2 of an hour is thirty minutes and 1/4 of an hour is fifteen minutes.

Having Fun with Fractions

Deb bought four flags for the parade. She spent 3 1/2 dollars (or $3.50) for each flag. She gave three of her four flags (or 3/4) to her friends. They held the flags in the parade. They marched for 1/2 of an hour (or 30 minutes). Deb and her friends had fun with fractions!

Glossary

equal   To be the same in size or number.

fraction   A part of a whole or of a whole number.

measure   To find out the size of something.

set   A group of things that go together.

whole   The total of all parts.

Index